W9-CPJ-488

POOP MEDICINE

Laura Loria

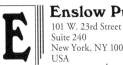

Enslow Publishing
101 W. 23rd Street
Suite 240
New York, NY 10011
USA

enslow.com

Words to Know

antibiotic A medicine that cures an illness caused by bacteria.

bacteria An organism that can carry disease.

diarrhea Poop that has usually become liquid.

digestive tract The system of organs in your body that break down food and get rid of waste.

donor A person who gives something to another person.

dung Animal poop.

feces Poop.

fertilizer A substance that helps plants grow.

intestine Tube-shaped organ that moves food through your digestive system.

procedure A series of steps for completing a specific task.

Contents

Poop All Around

Nature can be both beautiful and ugly. We have colorful flowers and messy weeds, but all things in nature have a purpose, even the weeds. Even the poop!

Poop is a part of nature that most people don't like to talk about. It is dirty and often has a bad smell. Your parents might tell you that it's not polite to talk about poop, but poop can be useful in many ways.

Throughout history, humans have used poop for lots of things. They have built houses with it and used it to fuel their cooking fires. Poop was the

FUN FACT

Poop is 75 percent water.

Poop is part of everyday life, for all creatures!

Animal poop contains energy that makes plants grow bigger.

original fertilizer, helping farmers grow food. People still use it today for fertilizer, building blocks, and rocket fuel.

Scientists can learn things about animals and people by examining their poop. Everyone's poop is unique, almost like a fingerprint. It shows what kind of things you eat and which types of bacteria are in your body. Scientists and doctors can use this information to treat illnesses. In some cases, poop itself is the cure! Doctors have found that poop can become a unique and important medicine.

Poop Treatments of the Past

Poop has been around as long as living things have existed on Earth. While people have used many plants as medicine, in some parts of the world, they used poop to heal and cure.

Ancient Egyptians believed that illnesses were caused by evil spirits. One of the cures they frequently used involved **dung**. It could be from humans or from animals, such as dogs or donkeys.

The Egyptians would mix the poop with other plants and herbs, packing

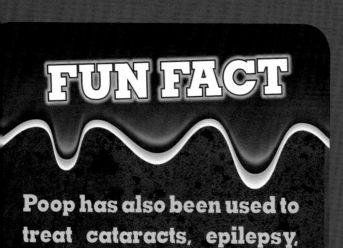

FUN FACT

Poop has also been used to treat cataracts, epilepsy, and nosebleeds!

In ancient times, people used what they found in nature for medicine, including poop.

Paintings of Egyptian gods show them using natural medicines.

or rubbing it onto the part of the body that hurt. These poop cures might have had some unexpected benefits, such as killing harmful kinds of bacteria.

Five hundred years ago in China, a doctor named Li Shinzen prescribed "yellow soup" to cure diarrhea, fevers, and other illnesses. The yellow soup was made of dried or aged poop, sometimes from a baby. The doctors thought the poop of a healthy person would cure a sick person, and they were right!

The Poop Cure

Most people do not like the idea of eating poop or rubbing it on their skin, even if it does work. The smell and taste of it might be worse than being sick! Today, doctors have found a way to use **feces** as medicine in clean, safe ways.

A fecal microbiota transplant involves moving one person's poop and helpful, healthy gut bacteria into another person's body to restore their digestive system to health.

FUN FACT

Healthy people poop anywhere from three times a day to once every three days.

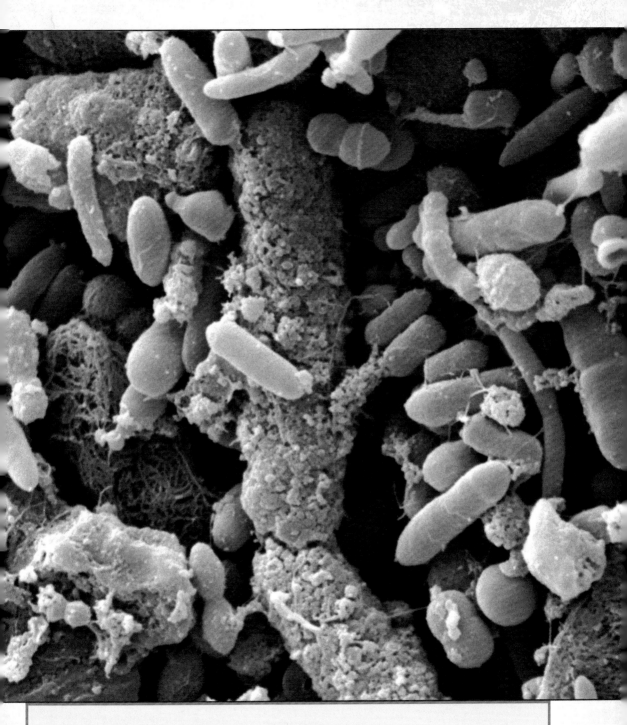

Poop contains many kinds of bacteria. Some can make you sick, but others can make you well.

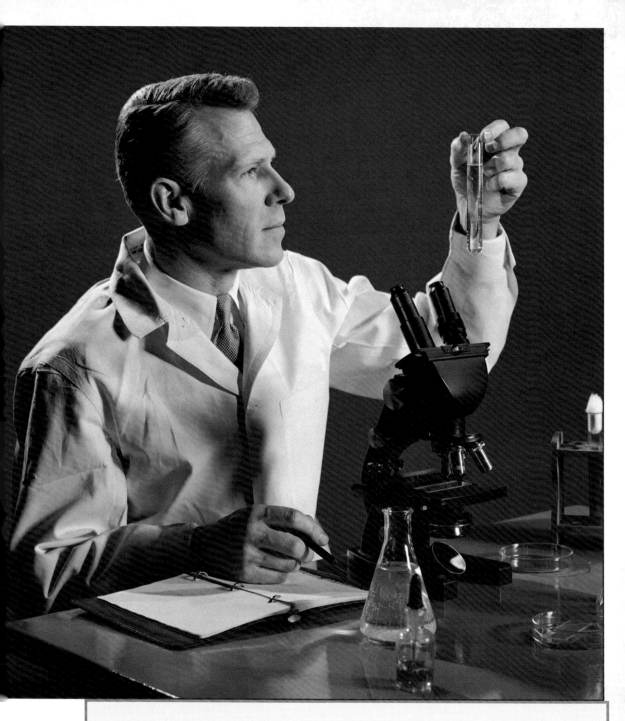

Scientists began using FMT (fecal microbiota transplant) on patients over seventy years ago.

Microbiota are the small organisms that live in your poop. They can eat the harmful bacteria that make a person sick and repopulate the good bacteria.

American doctors began using fecal microbiota transplant, or FMT, in the 1950s. There have been more than two hundred medical case studies on FMT. They show that between 92 and 95 percent of fecal transplants are successful. However, there are still very few doctors who do the procedure.

FUN FACT

With instructions from their doctor, some patients can do FMT at home.

Saving Lives

Poop cures have often been used to treat a variety of stomach problems. Today, fecal microbiota transplants are used in treating one particular illness, *Clostridium difficile* infection. It's shortened name is *C. diff*.

C. diff is a very serious disease. It's an infection, which means it contains bacteria that are harmful to humans. In 2012, 347,000 people in the United States had *C. diff*.; 14,000 of those people died from it.

Mostly older people get *C. diff*, but there are more and more young people who are diagnosed each year. Often, people get it after they have been in the hospital for another illness or after they have taken **antibiotic** medicines.

FUN FACT

C. diff can survive for up to ninety days on surfaces.

When people take antibiotics to kill bacteria like E. coli, sometimes they get *C. diff* infections.

C. diff affects the colon and other organs in the digestive tract. Patients with *C. diff* will have diarrhea, cramping, and fever. They may feel like throwing up and may become dehydrated. In the worst cases, it can damage a person's organs, leading to death.

Step by Step

Any medical treatment has a specific procedure. It is important to follow the procedure so that the treatment can do its job. The fecal microbiota transplant treatment has three steps.

The first step is collection. A stool sample is taken from a healthy person. The good bacteria in the healthy poop fights the bad bacteria that is making

FUN FACT

Doctors can freeze poop samples for up to two months!

Scientists wear goggles and gloves to protect themselves in the lab.

the patient sick. Doctors check the sample to make sure it is safe for transplantation.

The second step is preparation. Scientists have to prepare the sample soon after it is collected. They add saline, or salty water, to the poop. Then they blend it up. Finally, they strain it to remove lumps.

The final step is the transplant. One way is to put a tube, called an NG tube, into a patient's nose and down into the throat. It can also be transplanted through a tube that goes right to the intestines, or the poop can be put into a pill.

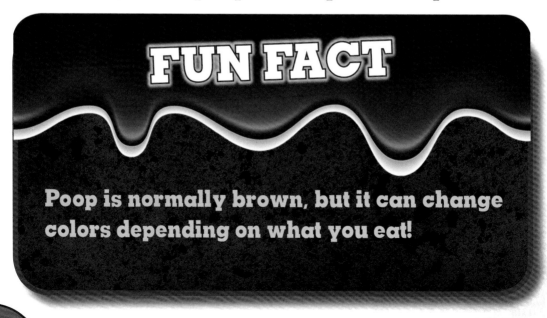

FUN FACT

Poop is normally brown, but it can change colors depending on what you eat!

These small tubes of poop are tested to discover what kinds of good bacteria they hold.

Poop Donors

Where do doctors get the healthy poop needed for fecal microbiota transplants? The best **donor** would be someone who lives with the patient because they would have been exposed to the same bacteria. When that isn't possible, the doctor can use donor poop.

Any healthy person can try to donate poop. They are examined by a doctor, who performs many tests. Not everyone's poop is right for FMT, though. At one donation center, only 40 out of 1,000 people were approved to donate their poop.

One donor can give up to five samples each week, and each sample can treat four different patients. The donor is paid $40 for each

FUN FACT

The average adult makes a pound of poop each day!

Poop donors have to answer many questions about their health before they can give samples.

donation. They get $50 if they complete a full week of donations. In a year, if all of the samples are accepted, that adds up to $13,000 for their poop!

Doggie Doo

Humans aren't the only ones who use fecal transplants to get well. Dogs with digestive problems are often put on a special diet or given probiotic medicines. However, some veterinarians are trying fecal transplants to cure dogs' tummy troubles.

Veterinarian Margo Roman read about human fecal microbiota transplants and thought that they might work for dogs, too. After all, she said, "Dogs eat poop anyway." Her first case was a poodle named Stovin, whose owners had tried many expensive treatments for his intestinal problems. Dr. Roman tried FMT, along with other treatments. Stovin got better quickly!

FUN FACT

"Coprophagia" is the word used to describe a dog's poop-eating habit.

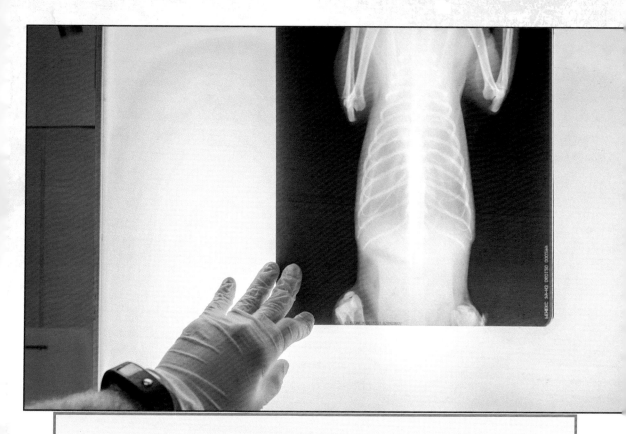

Animals can't tell us when they're sick, so veterinarians use tools like X-rays to examine them.

Since then, Dr. Roman has used FMT on many other pets. She even uses it to stop dogs from eating poop! She thinks that the dogs must want to eat the poop to make their tummies feel better, so she gives them a safe treatment of poop medicine. She says that the dogs no longer eat poop after the treatment.

Poop Beauty

Many skin treatments use natural ingredients, mostly from plants. One Japanese product used for beautiful skin is made of nightingale poop. It is called Uguisu No Fun. The poop is collected, cleaned, and dried into a powder. Then it is used in soaps, lotions, and masks.

Female Japanese performers called geishas used this beauty treatment hundreds of years ago. The poop contains guanine, which makes dark spots fade. It also has urea, which helps the skin keeps its moisture. A nightingale face treatment is said to make you look younger and have clearer skin.

These treatments are very expensive. The nightingale poop can only be found in

FUN FACT

A poop facial at one salon in New York costs $180.

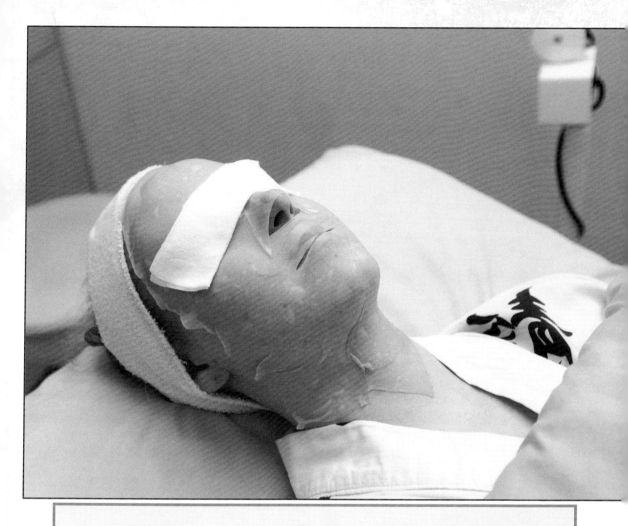

Some people pay to have bird poop smeared on their faces, in the hope that they will have better skin.

one place in the world, so it is rare. It comes from one type of bird found on the island of Kyushu. The nightingales are only allowed to eat berries and seeds, to keep the poop pure.

The Future of Poop Medicine

C. diff infection is only one of many types of gut problems. Doctors are hopeful that fecal microbiota transplants may be able to help people with other diseases, such as Crohn's disease or irritable bowel syndrome. They hope that the good bacteria will fight the harmful bacteria that cause the illness.

The usual treatment for illnesses is antibiotics, but they may make the problems

FUN FACT

Doctors think that poop medicine might help patients with multiple sclerosis, Parkinson's disease, and even bad breath!

Many people have trouble with their digestive system, and some diseases have no cure.

worse and can be expensive. Fecal microbiota transplant treatments cost very little and do not harm the patient.

Doctors are looking for other problems that poop medicine might be able to treat. They think that illnesses in other parts of the body might be

One day, FMT may replace antibiotics in treating some illnesses.

related to problems in the gut. If they treat the gut with fecal microbiota transplants, other illnesses might be cured as well.

Some children with autism have seen improvements in their symptoms after trying FMT. Their good behaviors got better, while their problem behaviors went down. They were also able to focus better and had more energy.

Learn More

Books

Gould, Francesca. *Why Dogs Eat Poop*. London, UK: G.P. Putnam's Sons Books for Young Readers, 2013.

Lawrence, Ellen. *Poop Cures*. New York, NY: Bearport Publishing, 2017.

Lawrence, Ellen. *The Scoop on Poop*. New York, NY: Bearport Publishing, 2017.

Woolf, Alex. *You Wouldn't Want to Live Without Poop*. London, UK: Franklin Watts, 2016.

Websites

Easy Science for Kids, "Bacteria: Good Guy or Bad Guy?"
easyscienceforkids.com/bacteria-good-guy-or-bad-guy
Is bacteria good or bad for us? It depends!

Easy Science for Kids, "The Excretory System"
easyscienceforkids.com/the-scoop-on-poop-human-excretory-system-basics
How does your body make poop? Let's find out!

The Ultimate Guide to Poop
healdove.com/misc/poop-2
Shapes and colors, your ultimate guide to poop.

Index

Published in 2018 by Enslow Publishing, LLC.
101 W. 23rd Street, Suite 240, New York, NY 10011

Library of Congress Cataloging-in-Publication Data

Names: Loria, Laura, author.
Title: Poop medicine / Laura Loria.
Description: New York : Enslow Publishing, 2018. | Series: The power of poop | Audience: Grades 3–5. | Includes bibliographical references and index.
Identifiers: LCCN 2017022372 | ISBN 9780766091139 (library bound) | ISBN 9780766091115 (pbk.) | ISBN 9780766091122 (6 pack)
Subjects: LCSH: Feces—Juveline literature. | Defecatication—Juvenile literature.
Classification: LCC QP159 .L67 2018 | DDC 612.3/6—dc23
LC record available at https://lccn.loc.gov/2017022372

Printed in the United States of America

To Our Readers: We have done our best to make sure all websites in this book were active and appropriate when we went to press. However, the author and the publisher have no control over and assume no liability for the material available on those websites or on any websites they may link to. Any comments or suggestions can be sent by email to customerservice@enslow.com.